GCSE Computer Science
Exam Practice Book
AQA GCSE 9-1

First published by Bao Books, part of Bao Group Limited, 2019

First Edition October 2019

Copyright © While Do Team 2019
Cover copyright © While Do Team 2019

Produced by: While Do Team
Contributors: Barnaby Tolhurst, JA Drinkwater, Winni Lam
Proofreader: Robert Welin

A catalogue record of this book is available in the British Library

ISBN 978-1-913130-00-8

Acknowledgements
Network topology icons reproduced by permission of Cisco Systems, Inc.
Cover image used under license from Shutterstock.com

If you want to let us know anything about this book, or to talk to us about Computer Science, please get in touch using the details below:
Bao Books
Bao Group Limited
PO Box 803
Borehamwood
WD6 9NN
United Kingdom

support@baogroup.ltd

Contents

1   Algorithms

1.1   Representing algorithms

1. Define the term **algorithm**.   (2 marks)

_____

_____

_____

2. Define the term **decomposition**.   (2 marks)

_____

_____

_____

3. Define the term **abstraction**.   (2 marks)

_____

_____

_____

4. Look at the following algorithm in pseudocode

```
1  numbers ← [1, 3, 5, 3, 8, 11, 10, 2]
2  output_value ← 0
3  FOR i ← 0 TO LEN(numbers) − 1
4    IF numbers[i] > output_value THEN
5       output_value ← numbers[i]
6    ENDIF
7  ENDFOR
8  OUTPUT 'result = ', output_value
```

   (a) Complete the following trace table for i, numbers[i] and output_value at the **end** of the for loop (line 7).   (3 marks)

i	numbers[i]	output_value
0	1	1

(b) What is the output of the algorithm? **(1 mark)**

_____

(c) Describe the purpose of the algorithm. **(2 marks)**

_____

_____

_____

5. Look at the following algorithm in pseudocode. You should assume that the values of a and b are always supplied as positive integers.

```
1  a ← USERINPUT
2  b ← USERINPUT
3  result ← 0
4  FOR i ← 1 TO a
5     tmp ← result + b
6     result ← tmp
7  ENDFOR
8  OUTPUT 'answer: ', result
```

(a) When the algorithm is used with a supplied as 5 and b is supplied as 2, its output is:

answer: 10

Complete the following trace table for the values of i and result **after** the assignment on line 6 for these values of a and b. **(3 marks)**

i	result
1	2

(b) What is the output of the algorithm when a is supplied as 3 and b is supplied as 5?

(2 marks)

(c) Describe the purpose of the algorithm.

(2 marks)

(d) Write an alternative algorithm with the same function that makes use of the ∗ (multiplication) arithmetic operation.

(3 marks)

6. Look at the following algorithm in pseudocode. You should assume that the values of a and b are always supplied as positive integers.

```
1  a ← USERINPUT
2  b ← USERINPUT
3  quotient ← 0
4  remainder ← a
5  WHILE remainder ≥ b
6     quotient ← quotient + 1
7     remainder ← remainder − b
8  ENDWHILE
9  OUTPUT 'answer: ', quotient, ' r ', remainder
```

(a) On which lines does the algorithm make use of input and output?

(1 mark)

(b) What is the output of the algorithm when a is supplied as 4 and b is supplied as 2?

(2 marks)

(c) Complete the following trace table for remainder and quotient when a is supplied as 5 and b is supplied as 2.

(3 marks)

remainder	quotient
5	0

(d) Describe the purpose of the algorithm.   **(2 marks)**

_____

_____

_____

1.2 Search algorithms

1. Look at the following pseudocode for a search algorithm.

```
1  SUBROUTINE search(search_array, search_term)
2    FOR i ← 0 TO LEN(search_array) − 1
3      IF search_array[i] = search_term THEN
4        OUTPUT 'found: ', search_term
5        RETURN
6      ENDIF
7    ENDFOR
8    OUTPUT 'not found: ', search_term
9  ENDSUBROUTINE
```

(a) Name the search algorithm shown.   **(1 mark)**

_____

(b) Explain the advantage of including a RETURN statement on line 5.   **(2 marks)**

_____

_____

_____

(c) The algorithm is used to search for a word in an array of words as follows

```
1  word_array = ['apple', 'banana', 'carrot', 'duck',
2                 'egg', 'fir', 'grape', 'horse']
3  search(word_array, 'grape')
```

i. What is the output of the algorithm?   **(1 mark)**

_____

ii. What is the maximum value of i during the execution of the algorithm?   **(2 marks)**

_____

iii. Another, more efficient algorithm could be used for the search. Name the algorithm and state the property of word_array that makes its use possible.   **(2 marks)**

_____

_____

2. Explain how the **binary search algorithm** works. **(4 marks)**

_____

_____

_____

_____

_____

3. A **binary search** is to be performed on an array of numbers. The array is shown below.

index	0	1	2	3	4	5	6	7
value	0	3	5	7	9	10	12	24

(a) What property of the array makes it suitable for a binary search? **(1 mark)**

_____

(b) The binary search is used to search for the number 12 in the array. The algorithm starts by comparing the search term, 12 with the value of the array at index 3.

   i. What is the value of the array at index 3? **(1 mark)**

_____

   ii. Explain which index the algorithm will use for the next comparison. **(2 marks)**

_____

_____

_____

   iii. How many comparisons **in total** will be made before the search term is found? **(1 mark)**

_____

   iv. How many comparisons would have to be made if the linear search algorithm was used instead? **(1 mark)**

_____

4. Explain and compare the advantages and disadvantages of the **linear search** and **binary search** algorithms.   **(6 marks)**

_____

_____

_____

_____

_____

_____

_____

_____

_____

_____

_____

1.3   Sorting algorithms

1. Explain how the **bubble sort** algorithm works.   **(4 marks)**

_____

_____

_____

_____

_____

_____

_____

2. Look at the following diagram which represents the first pass of the **bubble sort** algorithm being applied to an array of numbers. The shaded squares represent elements of the array that are being compared, and the arrows represent a pair of elements being swapped.

| Step 1 | **0** | **3** | 6 | 2 | 1 | 9 | 7 | 8 |

| Step 2 | 0 | **3** | **6** | 2 | 1 | 9 | 7 | 8 |

| Step 3 | 0 | 3 | **6** | **2** | 1 | 9 | 7 | 8 |

| Step 4 | 0 | 3 | 2 | **6** | **1** | 9 | 7 | 8 |

| Step 5 | 0 | 3 | 2 | 1 | **6** | **9** | 7 | 8 |

| Step 6 | 0 | 3 | 2 | 1 | 6 | **9** | **7** | 8 |

| Step 7 | 0 | 3 | 2 | 1 | 6 | 7 | **9** | **8** |

| End | 0 | 3 | 2 | 1 | 6 | 7 | 8 | **9** |

(a) Is the algorithm sorting in ascending or descending order?   **(1 mark)**

_____

(b) Explain why the pair of elements being compared in Step 3 must be swapped.
                                                                             (2 marks)

_____

_____

(c) During the first pass, seven comparisons are made. How many comparisons must be made during the next pass?   **(1 mark)**

_____

(d) How many passes in total must be made before it can be guaranteed that the array is in the correct order?   **(1 mark)**

_____

3. The following pseudocode is for the **bubble sort** algorithm. A subroutine, BubbleSort, is defined which performs the sort on an array of numbers, and returns the array of numbers in ascending order

```
1  SUBROUTINE BubbleSort(data_array)
2    FOR i ← 1 TO LEN(data_array) - 1
3      FOR j ← 0 TO LEN(data_array) - i - 1
4        IF data_array[j] > data_array[j+1] THEN
5          temp ← data_array[j]
6          data_array[j] ← data_array[j+1]
7          data_array[j+1] ← temp
8        ENDIF
9      ENDFOR
10   ENDFOR
11   RETURN data_array
12 ENDSUBROUTINE
```

(a) Write out a trace table for i, j, data_array when data_array is supplied as [4, 3, 1, 2]. **(3 marks)**

_____

_____

_____

_____

_____

_____

(b) Write out a trace table for i, j, data_array when data_array is supplied as [1, 2, 3, 4]. **(3 marks)**

_____

_____

_____

_____

_____

_____

(c) How could you modify the algorithm to make it more efficient at sorting arrays that are already in ascending order? **(2 marks)**

_____

_____

_____

4. Look at the following diagram which represents the **merge sort** algorithm being applied to an array of numbers. The diagram shows the original array being successively split into smaller sub-arrays, then the sub-arrays being successively merged and sorted into larger sub-arrays.

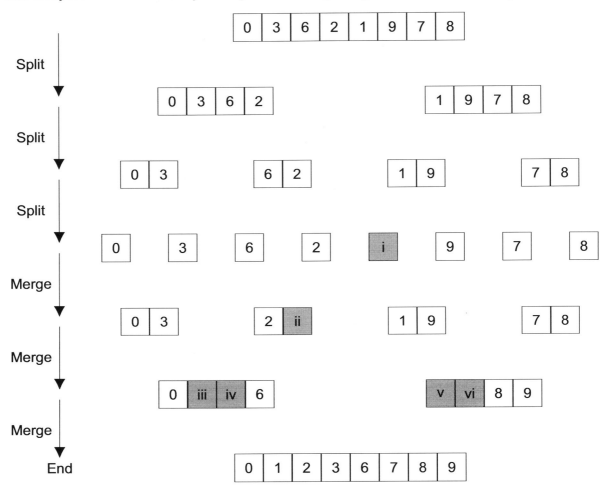

(a) Some of the array elements are missing numbers. The elements with missing numbers are shaded and marked i–vi in the diagram. Fill in the missing numbers below.

(4 marks)

i. _____   iv. _____

ii. _____   v. _____

iii. _____   vi. _____

(b) Explain why merge sort is more efficient than bubble sort.   **(3 marks)**

_____

_____

_____

_____

_____

(c) What is the disadvantage of the merge sort algorithm compared with bubble sort?

(1 mark)

_____

_____

2 Programming

2.1 Variables and data types

1. Define the term **variable declaration**.   **(2 marks)**

2. The following pseudocode excerpt contains an error. Explain why.

```
1  constant x ← 10
2  OUTPUT 'x = ', x
3  x ← 20
4  OUTPUT 'x = ', x
```

(2 marks)

3. The following code excerpt is from a program in a language that requires variables to be declared before they are used.

```
1  integer phone_number;
2  phone_number = '0209876142';
3  name = 'Kay';
4  OUTPUT 'name: ', name, '; number: ', phone_number;
```

Explain the **two** errors that the code excerpt contains.   **(2 marks)**

4. Choose the most appropriate **data type** to store each of the following values. You should choose from the following data types:

integer   real   Boolean   character   string
(4 marks)

   (a) 'one two three'   (b) 'o'

(c) `0`   (d) `5 MOD 2`

_____   _____

(e) `1.5 * 3`   (f) `1.5 < 3`

_____   _____

5. Which of the following statements about data types is false? Circle one letter only.

   (1 mark)

   A. Data types limit the type of data a function can take
   B. Data type systems help to identify type errors in programming
   C. Data types have the same names across all programming languages
   D. Data types affect the size of a variable in memory

6. Which of the following statements about variable names is false? Circle one letter only.

   (1 mark)

   A. Variable names can improve readability of a program
   B. A variable name must always start with a number
   C. Variable names cannot contain arithmetic or relational operators
   D. A variable's name can give extra information on how it is used in a program

7. The code excerpts in parts a) to d) are all intended to output the value of variable i 5 times. Inspect each one and answer the questions that follow.

   (a)
   ```
   1  integer i ← 0
   2  WHILE i = 5
   3     OUTPUT 'i = ', i
   4     i ← i + 1
   5  ENDWHILE
   ```

   i. Which line contains an error.   **(1 mark)**

   _____

   ii. Correct the line that contains the error in the space below.   **(1 mark)**

   _____

   (b)
   ```
   1  integer i ← 0
   2  WHILE i ≤ 5
   3     OUTPUT 'i = ', i
   4     i ← i + 1
   5  ENDWHILE
   ```

   i. Which line contains an error.   **(1 mark)**

   _____

   ii. Correct the line that contains the error in the space below.   **(1 mark)**

   _____

(c)
```
1  integer i ← 0
2  WHILE i < 5
3    OUTPUT 'i = ', i
4
5  ENDWHILE
```

i. Which line contains an error.   **(1 mark)**

ii. Correct the line that contains the error in the space below.   **(1 mark)**

(d)
```
1  real i ← 0
2  WHILE i ≠ (5.0/3.0)
3    OUTPUT 'i = ', i
4    i ← i + (1.0/3.0)
5  ENDWHILE
```

i. State whether or not there are any errors in this excerpt, and explain your answer.
                                                                   (3 marks)

2.2   Iteration and selection

1. Describe what is meant by the terms **definite iteration** and **indefinite iteration**.   **(2 marks)**

_____

_____

_____

2. WHILE...ENDWHILE and REPEAT...UNTIL loops are both examples of indefinite iteration. State the difference between these two types of loop.   **(2 marks)**

_____

_____

_____

3. For each of the following situations, state which of definite iteration or indefinite iteration would be the most suitable to use.   **(4 marks)**

   (a) Searching for a particular value in an array of numbers.

_____

   (b) Outputting every value in an array of numbers.

_____

   (c) Finding the maximum value in an array of numbers.

_____

   (d) Reading all the data from a file of unknown length.

_____

   (e) Playing a video on repeat until a user clicks the 'stop' button.

_____

   (f) Driving a robot forwards until it hits an obstacle.

_____

4. Look at the following code excerpt.

```
1  a ← USERINPUT
2  IF a < 2 THEN
3    OUTPUT 'a is smaller than 2'
4  ELSE IF a > 2 THEN
5    OUTPUT 'a is bigger than 2'
6  ELSE
7    OUTPUT 'a is equal to 2'
8  ENDIF
```

(a) State the line numbers of the selection statements.   **(2 marks)**

_____

(b) Explain the function of selection statements, using the code excerpt above as an example.
                                                                            (3 marks)

_____

_____

_____

_____

_____

_____

2.3 Arithmetic operations

1. Describe the difference between **real division** and **integer division**. (2 marks)

_____

_____

_____

2. State the function of the MOD operator. (1 mark)

_____

_____

_____

3. Write down the output of each of the following one-line programs. (4 marks)

   (a) OUTPUT 1 + (3 − 2)   (b) OUTPUT 5 MOD 2

   _____   _____

   (c) OUTPUT 5 DIV 3   (d) OUTPUT 5 / 2

   _____   _____

   (e) OUTPUT 1 + 2 * 3   (f) OUTPUT (5 DIV 2) * (5 MOD 2)

   _____   _____

2.4   Relational operations

1. Look at the following pseudocode representation of a program

```
1  OUTPUT 'Please enter a value for x'
2  x ← USERINPUT
3  OUTPUT 'Please enter a value for y'
4  y ← USERINPUT
5
6  IF x < y THEN
7     OUTPUT 'A'
8  ENDIF
9
10 IF x > y THEN
11    OUTPUT 'B'
12 ENDIF
13
14 IF x ≥ y THEN
15    OUTPUT 'C'
16 ENDIF
17
18 IF x ≠ y THEN
19    OUTPUT 'D'
20 ENDIF
21
22 IF y ≤ x THEN
23    OUTPUT 'E'
24 ENDIF
25
26 IF x = y THEN
27    OUTPUT 'F'
28 ENDIF
```

What is the output of this program when the input is as follows: **(4 marks)**

(a) x = 1, y = 2   (b) x = 2, y = 2

_____   _____

_____   _____

_____   _____

_____   _____

(c) x = 3, y = 1   (d) x = 'a', y = 'b'

_____   _____

_____   _____

_____   _____

_____   _____

2.5 String operations

1. Explain the difference between the string operations CHAR_TO_CODE and STRING_TO_INT.

   (2 marks)

   _____

   _____

   _____

   _____

   _____

2. Define the term **concatenation**.   **(1 mark)**

   _____

   _____

3. Write down the output of each of the following one-line programs.   **(4 marks)**

   (a) OUTPUT 'I LIKE ' + 'CHIPS'

   _____

   (b) OUTPUT CHAR_TO_CODE('B') – CHAR_TO_CODE('A')

   _____

   (c) OUTPUT SUBSTRING(4, 10, 'Seven substrings')

   _____

   (d) OUTPUT CODE_TO_CHAR(CHAR_TO_CODE('A') + LEN('string'))

   _____

   (e) OUTPUT POSITION('Seven substrings', 'n')

   _____

   (f) OUTPUT STRING_TO_REAL('1.5') + 10

   _____

2.6 Structured programming

1. Write a short description of the structured approach to programming.   **(3 marks)**

_____

_____

_____

_____

_____

_____

_____

2. Why is it important that program modules provide a clear, well documented interface?
          (2 marks)

_____

_____

_____

_____

_____

_____

_____

3. Describe the advantages of structured programming.   **(2 marks)**

_____

_____

_____

_____

_____

_____

_____

4. Look at the following program represented in pseudocode

```
1  SUBROUTINE MaxValue(data_array)
2    max_value ← data_array[0]
3    FOR i ← 0 TO LEN(data_array) − 1
4      IF data_array[i] > max_value THEN
5        max_value ← data_array[i]
6      ENDIF
7    ENDFOR
8    RETURN max_value
9  ENDSUBROUTINE
10
11 SUBROUTINE OutputMax(data_array)
12   max_value ← MaxValue(data_array)
13   OUTPUT 'maximum value is ', max_value
14 ENDSUBROUTINE
15
16 data ← [5, 4, 7, 3, 9, 10, 27, 13, 19]
17 OutputMax(data)
```

(a) Give an example of the use of a **local variable** in the program, and explain why this is preferable to using a global variable. **(3 marks)**

_____

_____

_____

_____

_____

(b) Write a technical description of the subroutine MaxValue. Your description should make reference to the subroutine's interface, what it is for, and any output. **(3 marks)**

_____

_____

_____

(c) Write a technical description of the subroutine OutputMax. Your description should make reference to the subroutine's interface, what it is for, and any output. **(3 marks)**

_____

_____

_____

2.7   Programming languages

1. State four reasons why high-level languages are more commonly used than low-level languages in writing computer programs.   **(4 marks)**

_____

_____

_____

_____

2. Describe the characteristics of machine code.   **(4 marks)**

_____

_____

_____

_____

3. (a) State the three types of program translator.   **(3 marks)**

_____

_____

_____

(b) Describe the main differences between the three types of program translator.

(4 marks)

_____

_____

_____

_____

_____

4. Draw lines to link the characteristics shown to the corresponding type of programming language.

(5 marks)

Fast execution

No compiling time

Better readability   High-level language

Precise processor control

Machine independent

Better memory efficiency

Difficult to maintain   Low-level language

Faster to develop

Easier to learn

2.8   Writing and understanding programs

1. The following pseudocode program generates a truth table for a NOT gate.

```
 1  OUTPUT 'Truth table'
 2  OUTPUT 'a  |  NOT a'
 3  FOR a ← 0 TO 1
 4    IF a = 0 THEN
 5       input_value_a ← True
 6    ELSE
 7       input_value_a ← False
 8    ENDIF
 9    IF (NOT input_value_a) THEN
10       result ← 1
11    ELSE
12       result ← 0
13    ENDIF
14    OUTPUT a, '  |  ', result
15  ENDFOR
```

The program's output is as follows

```
Truth table
a  |  NOT a
0  |  1
1  |  0
```

Rewrite the program so that it generates the truth table for an AND gate. Your program will need to iterate over two variables, a and b, and its output should be

```
Truth table
a  |  b  |  a AND b
0  |  0  |  0
0  |  1  |  0
1  |  0  |  0
1  |  1  |  1
```

(6 marks)

_____

_____

_____

_____

_____

_____

2. Logic circuits combine logic gates to take some binary inputs, and supply a binary output. Logic circuits can be modelled in code as expressions using the logical operators AND, OR and NOT to represent individual logic gates. For each of the following logic circuits, write down an assignment statement in pseudocode for the output, x, in terms of the inputs a, b.... The first one has been done for you as an example.

Example:

Answer: x ← a AND b

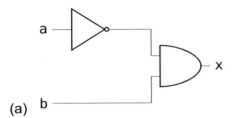

(a) b   **(2 marks)**

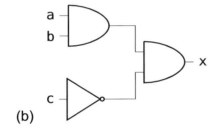

(b)   **(3 marks)**

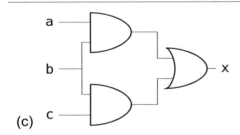

(c) c   **(3 marks)**

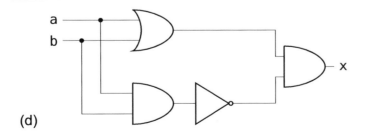

(d)   **(3 marks)**

3. A software engineer is writing a program to ask the user to input a character, then output whether the character lies in the first half of the alphabet (A-M) or the second half (N-Z). The software engineer has written the following pseudocode.

```
1  OUTPUT 'Please enter a character'
2  input_char ← USERINPUT
3  IF (input_char ≥ 'A') AND (input_char ≤ 'M') THEN
4    OUTPUT input_char, ' is in the first half of the alphabet'
5  ELSE
6    OUTPUT input_char, ' is in the second half of the alphabet'
7  ENDIF
```

(a) What would the output be when the user supplies the following inputs.   **(4 marks)**

   i. F

   _____

   ii. Q

   _____

   iii. f

   _____

   iv. &

   _____

(b) The software engineer realises that the program's output is inaccurate if the user inputs a lower case character or a character which is not a letter. Show how you would modify the pseudocode to fix these problems.   **(6 marks)**

   _____

   _____

   _____

   _____

   _____

   _____

   _____

   _____

   _____

   _____

   _____

   _____

4. (a) Write a pseudocode function called Is_lower, which takes a character as its input, and outputs True if the character is a lower case letter, or False if it is not.
       Start your pseudocode like this
           SUBROUTINE Is_lower(input_char)

       (2 marks)

    (b) Write a pseudocode function called Is_upper, which takes a character as its input, and outputs True if the character is an upper case letter, or False if it is not.
       Start your pseudocode like this
           SUBROUTINE Is_upper(input_char)

       (2 marks)

    (c) Write a pseudocode function called Is_letter, which takes a character as its input, and outputs True if the character is a letter, or False if it is not. Your function should call the functions Is_lower and Is_upper as described above.
       Start your pseudocode like this
           SUBROUTINE Is_letter(input_char)

       (2 marks)

5. A linguist wants to know which letters occur most frequently in the English language. The following pseudocode is for a program that generates and prints a table showing the number of times each of the letters A-Z appear in a string entered by the user. You have been asked to complete the pseudocode.

```
 1  frequency_table = [0, 0, 0, 0, 0, 0, 0, 0, 0, 0, 0, 0,
 2    0, 0, 0, 0, 0, 0, 0, 0, 0, 0, 0, 0, 0, 0]
 3
 4  OUTPUT 'Please enter some text'
 5  input_text ← USERINPUT
 6
 7  FOR i ← 0 TO LEN(input_text) − 1
 8    input_character ← input_text[i]
 9    IF input_character ≥ 'A' AND input_character ≤ 'Z' THEN
10      character_index ←  ?
11      frequency_table[character_index] ←  ?
12    ELSE IF input_character ≥ 'a' AND input_character ≤ 'z' THEN
13      character_index ←  ?
14      frequency_table[character_index] ←  ?
15    ENDIF
16  ENDFOR
17
18  OUTPUT 'Frequency Table:'
19  FOR i ← 0 TO 25
20    letter_code ← CHAR_TO_CODE('A') + i
21    letter ← CODE_TO_CHAR(letter_code)
22    OUTPUT letter, ':', frequency_table[i]
23  ENDFOR
```

The array frequency_table should contain the number of occurrences of each letter, with the number of occurrences of 'A' in element 0 of the array, of 'B' in element 1 of the array and so on, through to the number of occurrences of 'Z' in element 25. The program should treat upper case letters and lower case letters the same, and should ignore any characters in the input that are not letters.

(a) Complete the code on line 10 to assign the correct array index (0 for 'A', 1 for 'B' etc.) for an upper case character to the variable character_index. **(2 marks)**

_____

(b) Complete the code on line 11 to increment the value of frequency_table[character_index]. **(1 mark)**

_____

(c) Complete the code on line 13 to assign the correct array index for a lower case character to the variable character_index. **(2 marks)**

_____

(d) Complete the code on line 14 to increment the value of frequency_table[character_index]. **(1 mark)**

_____

6. Caesar's Cipher is an ancient technique for encrypting messages, in which each letter in a message is 'shifted' a certain number of places in the alphabet. For example, if the shift is 3, 'A' becomes 'D', 'B' becomes 'E' and so on. At the end of the alphabet, the shift wraps round to the beginning, so that 'X' becomes 'A', 'Y' becomes 'B' and 'Z' becomes 'C'. The message 'SEND MORE FOOD' becomes 'VHQG PRUH IRRG'

Look at the following pseudocode for a program that implements the cipher.

```
 1  OUTPUT 'Please enter a shift value between 1 and 25'
 2  shift ← USERINPUT
 3  OUTPUT 'Please enter some upper case text to encipher'
 4  input_text ← USERINPUT
 5  output_text ← ''
 6  FOR i ← 0 TO LEN(input_text) − 1
 7    input_character ← input_text[i]
 8    IF input_character ≥ 'A' AND input_character ≤ 'Z' THEN
 9      input_index ← CHAR_TO_CODE(input_character) − CHAR_TO_CODE('A')
10      output_index ← Apply_Caesar_shift(input_index, shift)
11      output_code ← output_index + CHAR_TO_CODE('A')
12      output_character ← CODE_TO_CHAR(output_code)
13    ELSE IF input_character ≥ 'a' AND input_character ≤ 'z' THEN
14      OUTPUT 'Error: only upper case text allowed'
15      output_character ← ''
16    ELSE
17      output_character ← input_character
18    ENDIF
19    output_text ← output_text + output_character
20  ENDFOR
21  OUTPUT 'Enciphered text: ', output_text
```

(a) Name the **string operation** used on line 19.   **(1 mark)**

_____

(b) The program asks the user to enter a shift value between 0 and 25. What happens if the user enters a value outside this range, and how could you improve the behaviour of the program in this case?   **(3 marks)**

_____

_____

_____

_____

_____

(c) The code on line 9 calculates input_index for a given input_character in the range A–Z. What is the value of input_index when input_character is 'A'?   **(2 marks)**

_____

(d) On line 10, the program calls a function, `Apply_Caesar_shift`. This function's arguments are the shift value, and the index of the character to shift. The function returns the shifted index. Pseudo code for the function is shown below.

```
1  SUBROUTINE Apply_Caesar_shift(input_index, shift)
2     output_index ←  ?
3     output_index ← output_index MOD 26
4     RETURN output_index
5  ENDSUBROUTINE
```

   i. Complete the assignment statement on line 2 to add the shift value to the input index.
(1 mark)

   ii. The code on line 3 is used to ensure that the output index remains within the range of 0-25. Explain why this method works. **(2 marks)**

7. The following pseudocode is for a program that prints a word randomly selected from an array of five words.

```
1  words ← ['Apple', 'Baboon', 'Celery', 'Dog', 'Egg']
2  index ← RAND_INT(0, LEN(words)-1)
3  OUTPUT 'Random word: ', words[index]
```

(a) Modify the program so that it prints five words selected at random from the array.

(2 marks)

_____

_____

_____

_____

_____

(b) Modify the program so that it prints each of the five words only once, in a random order. Your program may modify the contents of the array.   **(5 marks)**

_____

_____

_____

_____

_____

_____

_____

_____

3 Data representation

3.1 Number bases

1. List the digits that are used in the following number bases **(3 marks)**

   (a) Binary

   (b) Decimal

   (c) Hexadecimal

2. Which number base do computers use to represent all data and instructions? **(1 mark)**

3. Explain why hexadecimal is often a more appropriate choice of number base than binary or decimal when communicating ideas about computer science. **(3 marks)**

3.2 Converting between number bases

1. Convert the bit pattern `00100101` into hexadecimal. **(1 mark)**

2. Convert the bit pattern 01111100 into hexadecimal.   **(1 mark)**

3. Convert the bit pattern 00001100 into hexadecimal.   **(1 mark)**

4. Convert the bit pattern 01010101 into hexadecimal.   **(1 mark)**

5. Convert the bit pattern 01101110 into hexadecimal.   **(1 mark)**

6. Convert $7C_{16}$ into binary.   **(1 mark)**

7. Convert $4D_{16}$ into binary.   **(1 mark)**

8. Convert 13_{16} into binary.   **(1 mark)**

9. Convert $F5_{16}$ into binary. **(1 mark)**

10. Convert $A7_{16}$ into binary. **(1 mark)**

11. Convert 5_{16} into decimal. **(1 mark)**

12. Convert $A1_{16}$ into decimal. **(1 mark)**

13. Convert 99_{16} into decimal. **(1 mark)**

14. Convert $2A_{16}$ into decimal. **(1 mark)**

15. Convert DB_{16} into decimal. **(1 mark)**

16. Convert the decimal number 12 into hexadecimal.   **(1 mark)**

_____

_____

_____

17. Convert the decimal number 64 into hexadecimal.   **(1 mark)**

_____

_____

_____

18. Convert the decimal number 72 into hexadecimal.   **(1 mark)**

_____

_____

_____

19. Convert the decimal number 179 into hexadecimal.   **(1 mark)**

_____

_____

_____

20. Convert the decimal number 223 into hexadecimal.   **(1 mark)**

_____

_____

_____

21. The following bit pattern represents a binary number

    01100110

    Convert this binary number into decimal.   **(1 mark)**

    _____

    _____

    _____

22. The following bit pattern represents a binary number

    00101111

    Convert this binary number into decimal.   **(1 mark)**

    _____

    _____

    _____

23. The following bit pattern represents a binary number

    01011110

    Convert this binary number into decimal.   **(1 mark)**

    _____

    _____

    _____

24. The following bit pattern represents a binary number

    11011101

    Convert this binary number into decimal.   **(1 mark)**

    _____

    _____

    _____

25. The following bit pattern represents a binary number

    10010010

    Convert this binary number into decimal.   **(1 mark)**

    _____

    _____

    _____

26. Convert the decimal number 32 into binary.   **(1 mark)**

_____

_____

_____

27. Convert the decimal number 66 into binary.   **(1 mark)**

_____

_____

_____

28. Convert the decimal number 212 into binary.   **(1 mark)**

_____

_____

_____

29. Convert the decimal number 97 into binary.   **(1 mark)**

_____

_____

_____

30. Convert the decimal number 189 into binary.   **(1 mark)**

_____

_____

_____

3.3   Units of information

1. List the two values that a single bit can have.   **(1 mark)**

_____

2. How many bits are grouped to form a byte?   **(1 mark)**

_____

3. How many gigabytes are there in a terabyte?   **(1 mark)**

_____

4. A number of bytes can be described using a prefix, for example **kilo**byte. Which one of the following shows the numbers of bytes in **ascending** order?   **(1 mark)**

   A. 100 bytes, 1 kilobyte, 2000 megabytes, 1 gigabyte

   B. 100 bytes, 1 kilobyte, 1 gigabyte, 2000 megabytes

   C. 1 kilobyte, 1 gigabyte, 100 bytes, 2000 megabytes

   D. 100 bytes, 1 gigabyte, 2000 megabytes, 1 kilobyte

5. Express 3000 bytes in kilobytes.   **(1 mark)**

6. Express 256 TB in GB.   **(1 mark)**

7. Express 28000 bits in kilobytes.   **(2 marks)**

8. How much disk space would 2000 files of size 2 MB consume? Express your answer in GB.
                                                                                            (2 marks)

3.4   Binary arithmetic

1. Add the following two bit patterns of binary numbers **(2 marks)**

   ```
   10101010
   00010001
   ```

2. Add the following three bit patterns of binary numbers **(3 marks)**

   ```
   00101010
   00010010
   00010111
   ```

3. Add the following two bit patterns of binary numbers **(2 marks)**

   ```
   00111011
   00011001
   ```

4. Add the following three bit patterns of binary numbers **(3 marks)**

   ```
   00001110
   00011110
   00000111
   ```

5. Add the following two bit patterns of binary numbers **(2 marks)**

   ```
   00101011
   00101001
   ```

6. Add the following three bit patterns of binary numbers **(3 marks)**

   ```
   00101110
   00010110
   00010111
   ```

7. Explain the effect of a binary shift operation of two places to the left on a binary number.
   (1 mark)

8. Which of the following arithmetic operations is equivalent to a binary shift of 3 places to the right? **(1 mark)**

    A. multiplication by 8

    B. multiplication by 4

    C. division by 8

    D. division by 4

9. Apply a binary shift of 2 places to the right to the following bit pattern

    `01010111` **(2 marks)**

10. Apply a binary shift of 3 places to the left to the following bit pattern

    `11011011` **(2 marks)**

3.5 Character encoding

1. Describe what is meant by the term **character set**. **(2 marks)**

2. Explain, using an example, what character encoding is. **(3 marks)**

3. How many bits are used to represent a character in ASCII? **(1 mark)**

4. Complete the excerpt of the ASCII character encoding table shown below by filling in the missing character codes. **(2 marks)**

Character	Code
A	
B	
C	67
D	
E	

5. Describe the advantages and disadvantages of the Unicode compared with ASCII. **(2 marks)**

_____

_____

_____

_____

_____

_____

6. Emoji are pictographic characters that are used to represent emotions, places, people and things. Each year, new emoji are introduced. Explain why new emoji are represented using Unicode, and not ASCII. **(2 marks)**

_____

_____

_____

_____

7. Which one of the following describes the characters in Unicode that can be represented using ASCII? **(1 mark)**

    A. All Unicode characters

    B. The Unicode characters with code 0 to code 256

    C. The Unicode characters with code 0 to code 127

    D. No Unicode characters

3.6 Images

1. An image is to be represented as a bitmap. The width of the bitmap is 600 pixels, and its height is 400 pixels. How many pixels does the bitmap contain? **(1 mark)**

2. In bitmap images, what is meant by the term **colour depth**? **(1 mark)**

3. Look at the diagram below of a 8 x 8 black and white bitmap image.

Row 1
Row 2
Row 3
Row 4
Row 5
Row 6
Row 7
Row 8

(a) Row 2 is represented by the bit pattern 01010111. Which bit value represents a black pixel? **(1 mark)**

(b) Write down the bit pattern that represents row 4. **(1 mark)**

(c) Which row is represented by the bit pattern 10101010? **(1 mark)**

(d) What is the colour depth of the image? **(1 mark)**

(e) What is the size of entire bitmap image in bytes? **(2 marks)**

4. A drawing of a rainbow is to be represented as a bitmap image. Each pixel in the image can be one of 8 colours.

   (a) What is the colour depth of the image?   **(1 mark)**

   (b) The width of the image is 16 pixels, and its height is 8 pixels. Calculate the size of the image in bits.   **(2 marks)**

3.7 Sound

1. To be stored and processed on a computer, sound must be sampled. Explain why.

   (2 marks)

   _____

   _____

   _____

   _____

2. Define the term **sample** when applied to the storage of sound information on a computer.

   (1 mark)

   _____

   _____

   _____

3. A particular sound file has been sampled at a sampling rate of 44 kHz and with a sample resolution of 16 bits.

   (a) Define the terms **sampling rate** and **sample resolution**

   (2 marks)

   _____

   _____

   _____

   _____

   (b) What is the size in bits of 1 second of sampled sound at this rate and resolution?

   (2 marks)

   _____

   _____

   _____

   _____

   (c) The file captures 4 minutes of sound. Calculate the size of the file in megabytes.

   (2 marks)

   _____

   _____

   _____

   _____

(d) Explain what would happen to the number of samples and the file size if the sample resolution was changed to 8 bits per sample. **(2 marks)**

_____

_____

_____

4. A mobile phone ringtone is stored as sampled sound data. The ringtone is 5 seconds long.

(a) What is the size in bits of the ringtone if it is sampled at a rate of 5000 Hz and a resolution of 8 bits per sample? **(2 marks)**

_____

_____

_____

(b) Suggest two ways that the file size could be reduced, without changing the duration of the ringtone. **(2 marks)**

_____

_____

_____

3.8 Data compression

1. Describe what is meant by the term **data compression**.   **(2 marks)**

2. Which of the following are reasons why data compression might be used?   **(2 marks)**

   A. To represent data as a bit pattern
   B. To reduce the space consumed by data in memory or external storage
   C. To reduce the amount of data that must be sent across a network link
   D. To protect data by encrypting it

3. Explain how **run length encoding** is used to compress data represented as a bit pattern.

   (3 marks)

4. Use run length encoding to represent the following bit pattern
   `00010011000111`   **(2 marks)**

5. The following is a bit pattern represented using run length encoding
   `4 1, 4 0, 3 1, 1 0, 4 1`
   Write down the bit pattern that has been represented.   **(2 marks)**

6. Look at the following tree that represents a Huffman code derived from the message 'HAVE A BANANA'.

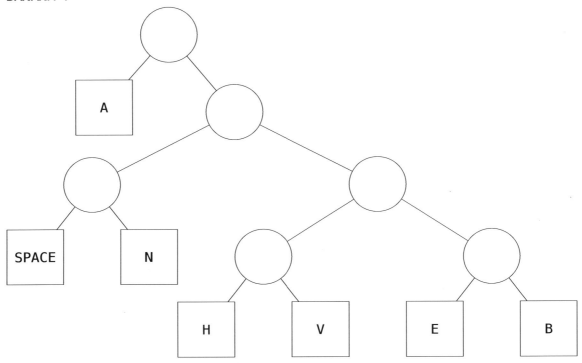

(a) Complete the following table showing the code for each character in the original message. Assume that a move to the left is represented by the digit 0, and a move to the right by the digit 1. **(4 marks)**

A	
SPACE	
N	101
H	
V	1101
E	1110
B	

(b) Write down the code for the message 'BE A BEAN'. **(3 marks)**

_____

_____

(c) Decode the following bit pattern using the tree shown above
1111010101010 **(3 marks)**

_____

_____

7. The message 'NEAT FEET' is being used to generate a Huffman code.

    (a) Complete the table below showing the frequency with which each character occurs in the message. **(2 marks)**

N	
E	3
A	1
T	
F	
SPACE	1

    (b) The following diagram shows a tree representation of the Huffman code for the message.

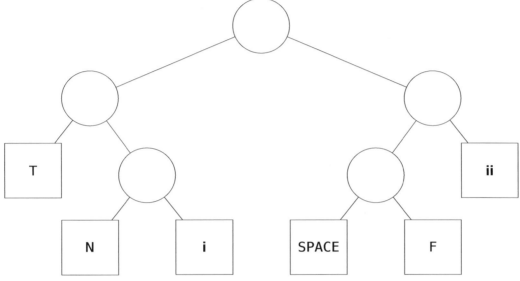

    Two of the nodes in the tree have been labelled **i** and **ii**. Fill in the characters that should appear in these nodes below. **(2 marks)**

    i. _____   ii. _____

    (c) Write down the code for the message 'NEAT FEET', and state how many bits are required to encode the message. **(3 marks)**

    (d) How many **more** bits are required to encode the message using ASCII? **(2 marks)**

4   Computer systems

4.1   Boolean logic

1.   Complete the truth table for the AND logic gate.   **(2 marks)**

A	B	A AND B
0	0	
0	1	
1	0	
1	1	

2.   Complete the truth table for the OR logic gate.   **(2 marks)**

A	B	A OR B
0	0	
0	1	
1	0	
1	1	

3.   Complete the truth table for the NOT logic gate.   **(1 mark)**

A	NOT A
0	
1	

4.   Draw the logic circuit for (NOT A) AND B.   **(2 marks)**

5. Draw the logic circuit for (A OR B) AND C.   **(2 marks)**

6. Draw the logic circuit for A AND NOT B.   **(2 marks)**

7. Complete the truth table for the following logic circuit.   **(3 marks)**

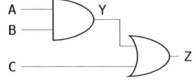

A	B	C	Y	Z
0	0	0		
0	0	1		
0	1	0		
0	1	1		
1	0	0		
1	0	1		
1	1	0		
1	1	1		

8. Complete the truth table for the following logic circuit.   **(3 marks)**

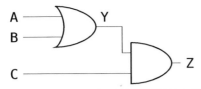

A	B	C	Y	Z
0	0	0		
0	0	1		
0	1	0		
0	1	1		
1	0	0		
1	0	1		
1	1	0		
1	1	1		

4.2 Hardware and software

1. Define the term **hardware**. (1 mark)

_____

_____

2. Define the term **software**. (1 mark)

_____

_____

3. Tick which of the following is hardware. (3 marks)

App ☐
Mouse ☐
Databases ☐
USB stick ☐
Keyboard ☐
Visual Display Unit ☐
Word Processing ☐
Spreadsheets ☐
Mobile Telephone ☐
Malware ☐

4. Give three examples of software usually used in business. (3 marks)

_____

_____

_____

5. Define the term **system software**. (1 mark)

_____

_____

6. Describe what is meant by **application software**. (2 marks)

_____

_____

7. State what the operating system manages.   **(5 marks)**

_____

_____

_____

8. Most operating systems include software called utilities. State four things that utilities usually look after.   **(4 marks)**

_____

_____

_____

_____

4.3   Systems architecture

1. Complete the following diagram by drawing lines from the names of the stages of the Fetch-Execute Cycle to the correct descriptions.

                                                                     (2 marks)

        FETCH   Interpret instruction code

        DECODE   Get next instruction code from
                                             main memory

        EXECUTE   Perform instruction

2. Explain the Fetch-Execute Cycle.   **(4 marks)**

_____

_____

_____

_____

_____

3. There are five things which make up Von Neumann architecture.

    Label the diagram appropriately.   **(5 marks)**

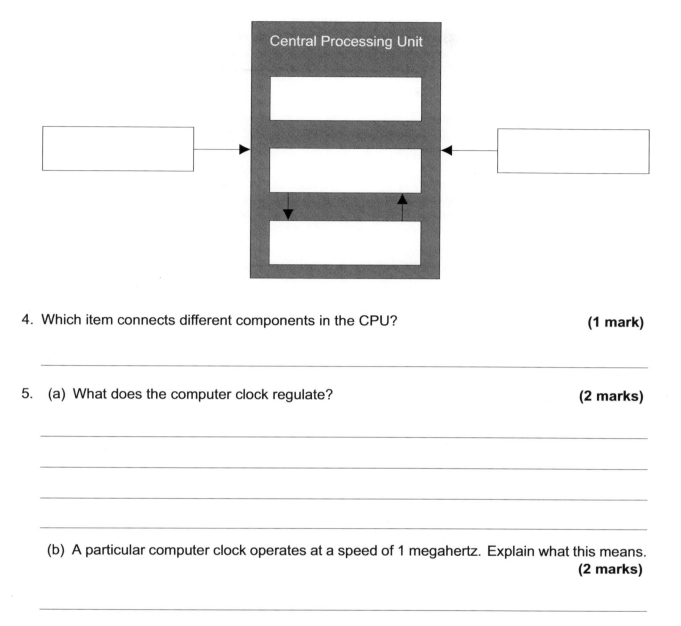

4. Which item connects different components in the CPU?   **(1 mark)**

_____

5. (a) What does the computer clock regulate?   **(2 marks)**

_____

_____

_____

_____

   (b) A particular computer clock operates at a speed of 1 megahertz. Explain what this means.
                    (2 marks)

_____

_____

_____

_____

6. Explain the effect of a dual core processor on the performance of the CPU   **(3 marks)**

_____

_____

_____

_____

_____

7. Explain the effect of cache size on the performance of the CPU.   **(3 marks)**

_____

_____

_____

_____

_____

8. Explain the different types of cache and the effect on the performance of the CPU.

(5 marks)

_____

_____

_____

_____

_____

_____

_____

_____

9. Define the term **cloud storage**.   **(2 marks)**

_____

_____

_____

_____

10. Tick the box next to each statement that describes an advantage in using cloud storage over local storage.   **(3 marks)**

faster access   ☐

cost effective   ☐

full control of access to data   ☐

scalable   ☐

easily maintainable   ☐

data safe from cyber attacks   ☐

data safe from local problems, e.g. power cut at home/office   ☐

11. (a) Explain what an **embedded system** is. **(2 marks)**

(b) Give two examples of something that uses an embedded system. **(2 marks)**

12. (a) Explain what a non-embedded system is. **(2 marks)**

(b) Give two examples of non-embedded systems. **(2 marks)**

13. Give an example of something that includes an embedded system found: **(6 marks)**

(a) on the motorway

(b) in the library

(c) at a car park

(d) in a supermarket

(e) in a skyscraper

(f) in an underground station

14. Explain the differences between embedded and non-embedded systems.   **(2 marks)**

_____

_____

_____

_____

15. State three kitchen items which would have embedded systems.   **(3 marks)**

_____

_____

_____

16. Some embedded systems in the home can connect to the Internet. Give one example of an embedded system that can do this.   **(1 mark)**

_____

_____

5 Networks

5.1 Network types and topologies

1. Define what a **computer network** is. **(1 mark)**

_____

_____

2. List three benefits of computer networks. **(3 marks)**

_____

_____

_____

_____

3. List three risks of computer networks. **(3 marks)**

_____

_____

_____

_____

4. (a) Put the following types of network in ascending order of the size of geographic area they cover.

LAN   **PAN**   **WAN**
(2 marks)

_____

_____

_____

_____

(b) Give two characteristics of one of the types of network listed above. **(2 marks)**

_____

_____

_____

_____

5. List two benefits of wireless networks against wired networks.   **(2 marks)**

_____

_____

_____

_____

6. List two risks of wireless networks compared with wired networks.   **(2 marks)**

_____

_____

_____

_____

7. (a) List two common network topologies.   **(2 marks)**

_____

_____

(b) Draw a topology diagram for one of the two network topologies you have listed above, assuming six hardware devices are in the network.   **(2 marks)**

(c) Choose one network topology from your answer to 7a, and list two advantages it has over the other network topology.   **(2 marks)**

_____

_____

_____

_____

8. Below are four network scenarios. Draw lines to link them to the most appropriate network topology.   **(4 marks)**

A company with a small budget
needs to network few computers

Star   A big enterprise with many
                                      machines

Bus   Access to data on some machines
                                      needs to be denied to others on
                                      the network

                                      Fast access to resources is
                                      required

9. Choose the disadvantage of using the bus topology from the following options.   **(1 mark)**

    A. expensive to install

    B. uses lots of cables

    C. hubs or switches required

    D. network fails when any device fails

    E. network performance decreases as the number of workstations increases

5.2   Network protocols and TCP/IP

1. (a) Define the term **network protocol**.   **(1 mark)**

_____

_____

(b) Match each network protocol below to its appropriate application.   **(5 marks)**

Ethernet   Allows secure web data
                                                communication

Wi-Fi   Reliably transfer data packets
                                                through the network

TCP   Addresses host interfaces

UDP   Defines what actions web devices
                                                should take in response to
                                                commands

IP   Used in WAN

HTTP   Unreliable but fast data
                                                transmission

HTTPS   Allows transfer files between a
                                                client and server on a network

FTP   Used in communication between
                                                email servers

SMTP   Receiving emails

IMAP   Compatible with smartphones

2. (a) State the four layers in the TCP/IP model.   **(4 marks)**

_____

_____

_____

_____

(b) State the main function of two of the layers.   **(4 marks)**

_____

_____

_____

_____

3. Match the following common network protocols to the TCP/IP layer that they operate on:

TCP

Wi-Fi   application layer

HTTPS

SMTP   transport layer

IP

Ethernet   internet layer

HTTP

FTP   link layer

UDP

IMAP

5.3   Network security

1. Give two reasons why network security is needed.   **(2 marks)**

_____

_____

_____

_____

2. Give two examples of the importance of network security.   **(2 marks)**

_____

_____

_____

_____

3. (a) State two network security methods.   **(2 marks)**

_____

_____

_____

_____

   (b) Describe each of the network security methods stated in your answer to 3a   **(2 marks)**

_____

_____

_____

_____

4. Below are four network security methods:
   authentication
   encryption
   firewall
   MAC address filtering

   (a) Explain, using an example, how a firewall works.   **(1 mark)**

_____

_____

(b) Explain how the four methods can work together to provide a greater level of security.

(2 marks)

_____

_____

_____

_____

5. Describe how MAC address filtering works.   **(3 marks)**

_____

_____

_____

_____

6   Cyber security

6.1   Fundamentals of cyber security

1. Define the term **cyber security**.   **(2 marks)**

_____

_____

_____

_____

2. (a) Define the term **social engineering**.   **(1 mark)**

_____

_____

(b) Give two examples of confidential information that might be obtained through social engineering.   **(2 marks)**

_____

_____

(c) Name four different social engineering techniques.   **(4 marks)**

_____

_____

_____

_____

3. Give two examples of how social engineering can be protected against.   **(2 marks)**

_____

_____

4. Define the term **blagging**.   **(2 marks)**

_____

_____

_____

5. Define the term **phishing**. (2 marks)

6. Define the term **pharming**. (2 marks)

7. Define the term **shouldering**. (2 marks)

8. (a) Define the term **malware**. (2 marks)

   (b) Give two examples of how malware can be protected against. (2 marks)

   (c) Name four different forms of malware. (4 marks)

9. Describe what a computer virus is. (2 marks)

10. Describe what a Trojan is in the context of malware.   **(2 marks)**

_____

_____

_____

11. Describe what spyware is.   **(2 marks)**

_____

_____

_____

12. Describe what adware is.   **(2 marks)**

_____

_____

_____

13. Give four examples of cyber security threats.   **(4 marks)**

_____

_____

_____

_____

14. Describe one scenario where misconfigured access rights would be a cyber security threat.
                                                                            (1 mark)

_____

_____

_____

15. Describe why removable media could be a cyber security threat.   **(1 mark)**

_____

_____

_____

6.2   Preventing cyber security threats

1. (a) Explain what penetration testing is.   **(2 marks)**

    _____

    _____

    _____

    (b) List the two types of penetration testing.   **(2 marks)**

    _____

    _____

    _____

2. (a) Describe the type of hacker white-box penetration testers are simulating.   **(2 marks)**

    _____

    _____

    _____

    (b) Name one vulnerability that white-box penetration testing is testing for.   **(1 mark)**

    _____

3. (a) Describe the type of hacker black-box penetration testers are simulating.   **(2 marks)**

    _____

    _____

    _____

    (b) Name one vulnerability that black-box penetration testing is testing for.   **(1 mark)**

    _____

4. (a) Name one advantage of using biometric measures to prevent cyber security threats.
                                                                                     (2 marks)

    _____

    (b) Name one disadvantage of using biometric measures to prevent cyber security threats.
                                                                                     (2 marks)

    _____

    (c) Describe three examples of commonly used biometric measures.   **(3 marks)**

    _____

    _____

    _____

5. Give three examples of security measures one can use to detect or prevent cyber security threats.   **(3 marks)**

_____

_____

_____

6. Explain how CAPTCHA works.   **(2 marks)**

_____

_____

_____

_____

_____

7 Ethics, the law and the environment

7.1 Ethical issues

1. In recent years, China has been implementing a computer system that gives every citizen a score based on their past behaviour.

   The system could be used to determine whether someone is able to:

   - decide whether a child should be admitted to a school based on parents' and relatives' scores
   - assess someone's past work history when they apply for a new job
   - approve loans based on past spending and borrowing habits
   - approve visa applications based on past violations
   - restrict the purchase or hire of cars based on economic status and traffic violation history
   - enhance an online dating profile with scores relating to economic status and social ratings from friends, family and past relationships

   (a) Suggest two benefits of this system. **(4 marks)**

   _____

   _____

   _____

   _____

   _____

   (b) Suggest two ethical issues with this system. **(4 marks)**

   _____

   _____

   _____

   _____

   _____

   _____

(c) Suggest two legal issues with this system.   **(4 marks)**

_____

_____

_____

_____

_____

_____

2. Self-driving cars and self-flying aeroplanes are being developed across the world. Investment in these types of vehicles is estimated to grow from tens of billions of pounds to hundreds of billions of pounds within the next decade.

   (a) Some self-driving cars are designed to be shared by several passengers, rather than to have a single owner. Describe two ways in which this could benefit the environment.
                                                                   (4 marks)

_____

_____

_____

_____

_____

_____

   (b) In order for these vehicles to be used in public, many laws and regulatory measures need to be introduced. Discuss two areas of regulatory and legal concern relating to self-driving vehicles.   **(4 marks)**

_____

_____

_____

_____

_____

_____

3. (a) Define the term **hacking**.   **(2 marks)**

_____

_____

_____

(b) Define the term **cracking**. **(2 marks)**

_____

_____

_____

(c) Draw lines to show which of the following characteristics relate to a hacker or a cracker. **(4 marks)**

Often break things

Usually knowledgeable about computer and internet security

Relies on existing tools to break into computer systems   Cracker

Breaks into systems for criminal intentions

Find weaknesses in computer security systems

Able to improve a computer system

Prevent crimes committed against a system   Hacker

Usually able to write computer programs

Exploit flaws in a computer system

4. (a) Describe two examples of how wearable technologies can be useful. **(4 marks)**

_____

_____

_____

_____

_____

(b) Data collected by wearable technologies often needs to be shared with companies making the technology for statistical analysis and product improvement. The collection and processing of this data is often not strictly regulated. Describe two ethical or legal concerns that might arise from this.   **(4 marks)**

_____

_____

_____

_____

_____

(c) Some wearable technologies are being developed into medical implants to monitor health conditions and prevent illnesses.

    i. Suggest one benefit of these implants.   **(1 mark)**

_____

_____

    ii. Suggest one area of concern about these implants.   **(2 marks)**

_____

_____

_____

_____

5. Current UK law includes sections outlining how copyright applies to computer programs.

(a) Describe the legal rights that copyright grants authors of a computer program.
                                                                                  (1 mark)

_____

_____

(b) State three things that copyright law allows the authors of a computer program to control
                                                                              (3 marks)

_____

_____

_____

(c) Some software is released under an open source licence, with the permission of the copyright holder. Describe the rights and responsibilities of users of open source software.

(2 marks)

_____

_____

_____

_____

6. Discuss the issues around the copyright of algorithms. Your answer should cover whether or not algorithms can be protected by copyright, and why, and any exceptions to this rule.

(8 marks)

_____

_____

_____

_____

_____

_____

_____

_____

_____

_____

_____

_____

_____

_____

_____

_____

_____

7. As high speed computer networks has become available to more people in society, cloud storage is now a popular way of storing data.

   (a) State three uses of cloud storage.   **(3 marks)**

_____

_____

_____

(b) Describe how cloud storage providers can impact the environment by how they manage their servers. **(4 marks)**

(c) State two legal concerns around the use of cloud storage. **(4 marks)**

8. Stealing computer code is illegal. For each of the following scenarios, give an example of software theft that could follow.

(a) Alex is a programmer working for a company that develops accounting software. He is about to change jobs to a competitor. **(1 mark)**

(b) Bethany really likes computer games. She discovers a computer program online that simulates a games console and can run files that are copies of existing games on the market. **(1 mark)**

(c) Charlie notices that there is a bug in the free trial of the computer program he has been using. The computer program continues to work after the trial has ended. **(1 mark)**

(d) Duncan started using code from an open source software project for his computer program. **(1 mark)**

9. Mobile technologies are convenient and, some argue, have brought people closer together. Discuss points of ethical and legal concern associated with mobile technologies.   **(8 marks)**

_____

_____

_____

_____

_____

_____

_____

_____

_____

_____

_____

_____

_____

_____

10. Contactless payment technology is increasingly commonly used.

    (a) State two places where contactless payments can be used.   **(2 marks)**

_____

_____

    (b) State two types of device that include contactless payment technology.   **(2 marks)**

_____

_____

    (c) Once set up, contactless technology is very easy to use for payments. Concerns about the safety and security of contactless payments have been addressed with various security measures. For each of the following concerns, explain the counter measure that exists to protect users.

       i. Accidentally spending too much money   **(1 mark)**

_____

_____

       ii. Accidentally making multiple payments   **(1 mark)**

_____

_____

       iii. Lost or stolen cards or devices being used to make purchases.   **(1 mark)**

_____

_____

11. (a) Describe four examples of how technology can cause damage to the environment.

                                                                            (4 marks)

_____

_____

_____

_____

_____

_____

_____

_____

    (b) Describe four areas where technology can be used to improve the environment.

(4 marks)

_____

_____

_____

_____

_____

_____

_____

_____

(4 marks)

8 Answers

1 Algorithms

1.1 Representing algorithms

1. An algorithm is a sequence of steps that can be followed to complete a task.

2. Decomposition is breaking a problem into a number of sub-problems, so that each sub-problem accomplishes an identifiable task.

3. Abstraction is the process of removing unnecessary detail from a problem.

4. (a)

i	numbers[i]	output_value
0	1	1
1	3	3
2	5	5
3	3	5
4	8	8
5	11	11
6	10	11
7	2	11

(b) `result = 11`

(c) The algorithm finds and outputs the maximum value of the array of numbers, `numbers`.

5. (a)

i	result
1	2
2	4
3	6
4	8
5	10

(b) `answer: 15`

(c) The algorithm calculates a x b and outputs the answer

(d)
```
1  a ← USERINPUT
2  b ← USERINPUT
3  OUTPUT 'answer: ', a*b
```

6. (a) Lines 1, 2 and 9

(b) `answer: 2 r 0`

(c)

remainder	quotient
5	0
3	1
1	2

(d) The algorithm calculates the quotient and remainder of dividing a by b and outputs the answer

1.2 Search algorithms

1. (a) Linear search algorithm

   (b) The RETURN statement stops the search in the case that search term has been found in the array. This improves the efficiency of the algorithm.

   (c) i. found: grape

       ii. 6

       iii. The binary search algorithm could be used because word_array is in alphabetical order.

2. The binary search algorithm requires the list to search in to be in [ascending/descending] order. The algorithm checks the middle item of the list to see if it is greater or less than the search term. If it is less than the search term, the search continues in the upper half of the list; if it is greater, the lower half. This process continues, successively halving the number of items to search until a single item is found.

3. (a) It is in numerical order / It has been sorted

   (b) i. 7

       ii. It will use index 5, as this is the middle of the upper part of the array.

       iii. 3

       iv. 7

4. The linear search algorithm can be used to search in any list or array, but the binary search algorithm requires that the data to be searched has already been sorted.
   The linear search algorithm is very simple to implement, but it is less efficient than the binary search algorithm. This is because the binary search algorithm works by successively dividing the search data in half, meaning that many fewer items of data need to be searched through.

1.3   Sorting algorithms

1. The bubble sort algorithm works by comparing the first and second items in a list/array, and swapping the first and second items if they are in the wrong order. This process is repeated on the second and third items, and so on, until the end of the list is reached. At this point, the last item in the list will be in the correct place. The whole process is then repeated up to the last but one item, and so on, until the entire list is in the correct order.

2. (a) Ascending.

   (b) They must be swapped because the first element is greater than the second, which is the wrong order.

   (c) Six.

   (d) Seven.

3. (a)

i	j	data_array
1	0	[3, 4, 1, 2]
1	1	[3, 1, 4, 2]
1	2	[3, 1, 2, 4]
2	0	[1, 3, 2, 4]
2	1	[1, 2, 3, 4]
3	0	[1, 2, 3, 4]

   (b)

i	j	data_array
1	0	[1, 2, 3, 4]
1	1	[1, 2, 3, 4]
1	2	[1, 2, 3, 4]
2	0	[1, 2, 3, 4]
2	1	[1, 2, 3, 4]
3	0	[1, 2, 3, 4]

(c) A Boolean flag could be used to track whether any swaps have been made in the inner loop. If no swaps have been made, the array is in ascending order, and a RETURN statement could be used to exit the subroutine early.

4. (a)   i. 1
         ii. 6
        iii. 2
        iv. 3
         v. 1
        vi. 7

(b) The algorithm works by dividing the data to be sorted into smaller lists/arrays, and sorting these smaller lists as they are merged back together. Merging lists that are already sorted is much more efficient than attempting to sort an entire, unsorted list, which is what the bubble sort algorithm does.

(c) It is harder to implement.
A well implemented bubble sort might perform better than a merge sort if the data to be sorted are already mostly in order.

2   Programming

2.1   Variables and data types

1. Variable declaration is a type of programming statement in which a variable's name and data type are specified before its first use

2. The variable x is declared `constant`, which means its value cannot be changed during the execution of the program. The assignment statement on line 3 attempts to modify x, which is an error.

3. The assignment statement on line 2 assigns a string to a variable that has been declared as an integer. The assignment statement on line 3 makes use of a variable before it has been declared.

4. (a) `string`
   (b) `character`
   (c) `integer` or `real`
   (d) `integer` or `real`
   (e) `real`
   (f) `Boolean`

5. C.

6. B.

7. (a)   i. Line 2
         ii. `WHILE i < 5`
   (b)   i. Line 2
         ii. `WHILE i < 5`
   (c)   i. Line 4
         ii. `i ← i + 1`

(d)   i. **Either:** Yes, because of the possibility of rounding errors, i might never equal 5/3 exactly, so the WHILE loop will continue forever.
Or: No, after 5 iterations of the WHILE loop, i will equal 5/3 exactly, and the loop will exit.

2.2   Iteration and selection

1. Definite iteration is the repetition of a section of code for a predetermined number of times. Indefinite iteration is the repetition of a section of code until a certain condition is met

2. A WHILE...ENDWHILE loop checks for the exit condition at the beginning of the loop, whereas a REPEAT...UNTIL loop checks for the exit condition at the end of the loop

3. (a) indefinite

   (b) definite

   (c) definite

   (d) indefinite

   (e) indefinite

   (f) indefinite

4. (a) lines 2, 4 and 6

   (b) A selection statement chooses which path of code to execute based on the logical expression within the selection statement. For example, the IF statement on line 2 has the condition a < 2. If this condition is true, line 3 gets executed and the program outputs a is smaller than 2. If it is false, line 4 is executed, which is another selection statement. If this statement's condition is true, line 5 is executed. If neither of the conditions are true, the ELSE statement on line 6 means that line 7 will be exectued.

2.3   Arithmetic operations

1. In real division, the result of dividing one number by another is expressed as a decimal.
In integer division, the result of dividing one number by another is expressed as an integer **quotient**, and an integer **remainder**.

2. The MOD operator returns the remainder after dividing one integer by another.

3. (a) 2

   (b) 1

   (c) 1

   (d) 2.5

   (e) 7

   (f) 2

2.4   Relational operations

1. (a) A
      D

(b) C
  E
  F

(c) B
  C
  D
  E

(d) A
  D

2.5   String operations

1. The operation CHAR_TO_CODE is a function which takes a character as its parameter and returns the corresponding ASCII code. The operation STRING_TO_INT is a function that takes a string as its parameter and if the string is a valid representation of an integer, returns that integer.

2. Concatenation is the operation that joins two strings together.

3. (a) I LIKE CHIPS
   (b) 1
   (c) n subs
   (d) G
   (e) 4
   (f) 11.5

2.6   Structured programming

1. Structured programming makes use of the three basic control structures (sequence, selection and iteration) and of subroutines. Common bits of code are organised in modules, sets of subroutines with clear, well documented interfaces (input parameters and return values).

2. It is important so that programmers can make use of modules without a detailed understanding of the way in which the modules are implemented, and so that tests can be written which adequately test the modules' functionality

3. Structured programming results in code that is easier to understand, test and debug

4. (a) Subroutine MaxValue uses a local variable max_value (e.g. line 2). Subroutine OutputMax uses a local variable max_value (e.g. line 12). The use of local variables in a subroutine, where possible, is preferable because it means that the subroutine can change the value of the variable without having any effect on the rest of the program.
   (b) Subroutine MaxValue takes a single array, data_array, as its input. It finds the maximum value of the array, and returns this value.
   (c) Subroutine OutputMax takes a single array, data_array, as its input. It finds the maximum value of the array, and outputs this value. It has no return value.

2.7   Programming languages

1. Any four of:

easier to read

easier to learn

programs are easier to debug

programs are easier to maintain

easier to adapt programs to run on different types of machine

2. All programming code written in high-level or assembly languages must be translated into machine code.
Machine code is expressed in binary.
Processors execute machine code, each type of processor has its own specific machine code instruction set.

3. (a) Interpreter, compiler and assembler

   (b) An interpreter translates high level language source code line by line into machine code and executes them immediately after translation.
   A compiler translates the entire source code of a program written in high level language into machine code.
   An assembler translates a program written in assembly language to machine code. This is different from a compiler, because assembly language corresponds 1:1 with machine code, so no further processing is required.

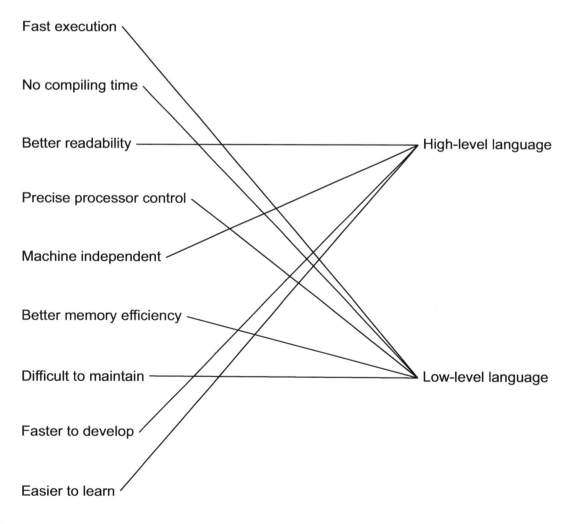

4.

2.8 Writing and understanding programs

1.
```
 1  OUTPUT 'Truth table'
 2  OUTPUT 'a  |  b  |  a AND b'
 3  FOR a ← 0 TO 1
 4    IF a = 0 THEN
 5      input_value_a ← True
 6    ELSE
 7      input_value_a ← False
 8    ENDIF
 9    FOR b ← 0 TO 1
10      IF b = 0 THEN
11        input_value_b ← True
12      ELSE
13        input_value_b ← False
14      ENDIF
15
16      IF (input_value_a AND input_value_b) THEN
17        result ← 1
18      ELSE
19        result ← 0
20      ENDIF
21      OUTPUT a, '  |  ', b, '  |  ', result
22    ENDFOR
23  ENDFOR
```

2. (a) x ← (NOT a) AND b

   (b) x ← (a AND b) AND (NOT c)

   (c) x ← (a AND b) OR (b AND c)

   (d) x ← (a OR b) AND NOT (a AND b)

3. (a)   i. F is in the first half of the alphabet
        ii. Q is in the second half of the alphabet
       iii. f is in the second half of the alphabet
        iv. & is in the second half of the alphabet

   (b)
```
 1  OUTPUT 'Please enter a character'
 2  input_char ← USERINPUT
 3  IF ((input_char ≥ 'A') AND (input_char ≤ 'M'))
 4      OR ((input_char ≥ 'a') AND (input_char ≤ 'm')) THEN
 5    OUTPUT input_char, ' is in the first half of the alphabet'
 6  ELSE IF ((input_char ≥ 'N') AND (input_char ≤ 'Z'))
 7      OR ((input_char ≥ 'n') AND (input_char ≤ 'z')) THEN
 8    OUTPUT input_char, ' is in the second half of the alphabet'
 9  ELSE
10    OUTPUT input_char, ' is not a letter'
11  ENDIF
```

4. (a)
```
 1  SUBROUTINE Is_lower(input_char)
 2    RETURN (input_char ≥ 'a') AND (input_char ≤ 'z')
 3  ENDSUBROUTINE
```

   (b)
```
 1  SUBROUTINE Is_upper(input_char)
 2    RETURN (input_char ≥ 'A') AND (input_char ≤ 'Z')
 3  ENDSUBROUTINE
```

(c)
```
1 SUBROUTINE Is_letter(input_char)
2   RETURN Is_upper(input_char) OR Is_lower(input_char)
3 ENDSUBROUTINE
```

5. (a) `character_index ← CHAR_TO_CODE(input_character) - CHAR_TO_CODE('A')`

   (b) `frequency_table[character_index] ← frequency_table[character_index] + 1`

   (c) `character_index ← CHAR_TO_CODE(input_character) - CHAR_TO_CODE('a')`

   (d) `frequency_table[character_index] ← frequency_table[character_index] + 1`

6. (a) concatenation

   (b) The program would continue to execute, potentially causing incorrect output later on. An IF statement could be used after the input has been read to check that the value is in range, and warn the user and abort the program if it is not

   (c) 0

   (d) i. `output_index ← input_index + shift`

   ii. The MOD operator returns the remainder of dividing the first argument by the second. The remainder can never be greater than or equal to the second argument, or less than zero, therefore `output_index MOD 26` will always be less than 26 and greater than zero.

7. (a)
```
1 words ← ['Apple', 'Baboon', 'Celery', 'Dog', 'Egg']
2 FOR i ← 1 TO 5
3   index ← RAND_INT(0, LEN(words)-1)
4   OUTPUT 'Random word: ', words[index]
5 ENDFOR
```

For example:

   (b)
```
1 words ← ['Apple', 'Baboon', 'Celery', 'Dog', 'Egg']
2 FOR i ← 0 TO 4
3   index ← RAND_INT(i, LEN(words)-1)
4   OUTPUT 'Random word: ', words[index]
5   words[index] ← words[i]
6 ENDFOR
```

Or:
```
1 words ← ['Apple', 'Baboon', 'Celery', 'Dog', 'Egg']
2 FOR i ← 1 TO 5
3   REPEAT
4     index ← RAND_INT(i, LEN(words)-1)
5   UNTIL words[index] ≠ ''
6   OUTPUT 'Random word: ', words[index]
7   words[index] ← ''
8 ENDFOR
```

3 Data representation

3.1 Number bases

1. (a) 0, 1

   (b) 0, 1, 2, 3, 4, 5, 6, 7, 8, 9

(c) 0, 1, 2, 3, 4, 5, 6, 7, 8, 9, A, B, C, D, E, F

2. Binary

3. Hexadecimal is a better choice than binary because it is a more compact representation that is easier to read and write (a byte is represented by two digits rather than 8). It is a better choice than decimal because each hexadecimal digit represents exactly 4 binary digits, which makes it easy to convert between binary and hexadecimal. This is important because computers use binary for all data and instructions internally.

3.2   Converting between number bases

1. 25_{16}

2. $7C_{16}$

3. $0C_{16}$

4. 55_{16}

5. $6E_{16}$

6. 01111100

7. 01001101

8. 00010011

9. 11110101

10. 10100111

11. 5

12. 161

13. 153

14. 42

15. 219

16. C_{16}

17. 40_{16}

18. 48_{16}

19. $B3_{16}$

20. DF_{16}

21. 102

22. 47

23. 94

24. 221

25. 146

26. 100000

27. `1000010`

28. `11010100`

29. `1100001`

30. `10111101`

3.3 Units of information

1. `0` and `1`

2. 8

3. 1000

4. B.

5. 1000 bytes in a kilobyte; 3000/1000 = **3 KB**

6. 1000 GB in a TB; 256x1000 = **256 000 GB**

7. 8 bits per byte, 28000/8 = 3500 bytes; 1000 bytes in a kilobyte, 3500/1000 = **3.5 KB**

8. 2000x2 MB = 4000 MB; 1000 MB per GB, 4000/1000 = **4GB**

3.4 Binary arithmetic

1. `10111011`

2. `01010011`

3. `01010100`

4. `00110011`

5. `01010100`

6. `01011011`

7. A binary shift of two places to the left will result in each digit in the number's bit pattern being moved two places to the left, and two 0 digits being inserted at the right of the number. (Accept multiplication by 4)

8. C.

9. `00010101`

10. `01101100`

3.5 Character encoding

1. A character set is a collection of characters (e.g. letters, numbers and punctuation) that can be used to write text in one or more languages.

2. Character encoding is the process of representing a set of characters (e.g. letters, numbers and punctuation), as a corresponding set of numerical codes, one for each character. This enables characters to be converted to codes and vice versa.
   An example is ASCII, which maps 128 letters, numbers, symbols and control characters onto 7 bit codes. (Alternative example: Unicode)

3. 7

4.

Character	Code
A	65
B	66
C	67
D	68
E	69

5. Unicode can represent many thousands of characters, covering all world languages, whereas ASCII is limited to 128 characters, covering only the English language.

   Unicode characters require more space than ASCII characters.

6. ASCII can only encode 128 characters, and these characters are already specified, so there is no space in the set for new emoji. Unicode can encode many thousands of characters, and there is space within the set for new characters, such as emoji.

7. C.

3.6   Images

1. number of pixels = width x height; 600 x 400 = **240 000 pixels**

2. The colour depth is the number of bits used to represent each pixel.

3. (a) 1
   (b) `01010011`
   (c) Row 3
   (d) 1
   (e) 8 bits per row gives 1 byte; 8 rows * 1 byte gives **8 bytes**

4. (a) 3
   (b) number of pixels = width x height = 16 x 8 = 128 pixels; 3 bits per pixel; size = bits per pixel x number of pixels = 3 * 128 = **384 bits**

3.7   Sound

1. Sound waves are recorded as analogue signals, which means they are continuous in level and time. Since computers can only store and process finite numerical information, the sound signals must be sampled, converted to a series of numbers.

2. A sample is a measure of the amplitude of a sound wave at a particular point in time.

3. (a) The sampling rate is the number of samples that are taken per second.
      The sample resolution is the number of bits used for each sample.
   (b) size in bits = time x rate x resolution
      size = 1 x 44000 x 16 = **704000 bits**

(c) size in bits = time x rate x resolution = 4 x 60 x 44000 x 16 = 168960000 bits

size in MB = size in bits / (8 x 1000000) = **21.12 MB**

(d) The number of samples would stay the same, because the sample rate has not changed. The file size would halve, because each sample would only consume 8 bits instead of 16.

4. (a) size in bits = time x rate x resolution

size = 5 x 5000 x 8 = **200000 bits**

(b) Any two from

use a lower sampling rate

use a lower sample resolution

use compression

3.8 Data compression

1. Data compression refers to a set of techniques that are used to reduce the number of bits required to represent particular data.

2. B. C.

3. When using run length encoding to compress a bit pattern, series of consecutive ones or zeros called runs are identified in the source bit pattern. Each run is represented by a number indicating the length of the run, and a 1 or a 0 indicating whether it is a run of ones or zeroes. Therefore, a run of length n can be represented by two numbers instead of n, which takes less space.

4. 3 0, 1 1, 2 0, 2 1, 3 0, 3 1

5. 1111000011101111

6. (a)

A	0
SPACE	100
N	101
H	1100
V	1101
E	1110
B	1111

(b) 111111101000100111111100101

(c) BANANA

7. (a)

N	1
E	3
A	1
T	2
F	1
SPACE	1

(b) i. A

ii. E

(c) 0101101100100101111100, 22 bits required

(d) For ASCII, 9 characters in message, 7 bits per character gives 7x9 = 63 bits

63 bits - 22 bits = 41 bits

41 bits more

4 Computer systems

4.1 Boolean logic

1.

A	B	A AND B
0	0	0
0	1	0
1	0	0
1	1	1

2.

A	B	A OR B
0	0	0
0	1	1
1	0	1
1	1	1

3.

A	NOT A
0	1
1	0

4.

5.

6.

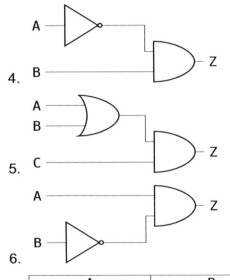

7.

A	B	C	Y	Z
0	0	0	0	0
0	0	1	0	1
0	1	0	0	0
0	1	1	0	1
1	0	0	0	0
1	0	1	0	1
1	1	0	1	1
1	1	1	1	1

8.

A	B	C	Y	Z
0	0	0	0	0
0	0	1	0	0
0	1	0	1	0
0	1	1	1	1
1	0	0	1	0
1	0	1	1	1
1	1	0	1	0
1	1	1	1	1

4.2 Hardware and software

1. Hardware is any physical component that makes up the computer.

2. Software is any program that runs on the computer.

3.

App	
Mouse	✓
Databases	
USB stick	✓
Keyboard	✓
Visual Display Unit	✓
Word Processing	
Spreadsheets	
Mobile Telephone	✓
Malware	

4. Any three from

> Word Processing
> Spreadsheet
> Payroll
> Accounts
> Mobile Phone Apps
> Air Traffic Control
> etc

5. These are programs that enable the computer to work.

6. These are programs installed on the computer that enable the user to perform a task. An example would be using word processing software to write a letter.

7. Security
   Input/Output Devices
   Memory
   Processor
   Software Applications

8. Any four from

> Security – encryption software
> Disk organisation – organise files into folders
> Data compression
> File back up
> etc

4.3 Systems architecture

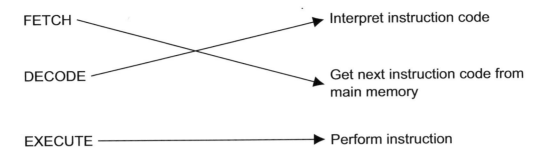

1.

2. The control unit fetches an instruction or data from a register, then it decodes the instruction or data. The arithmetic logic unit carries out logical or arithmetic operations. The fetch-execute cycle does this repeatedly.

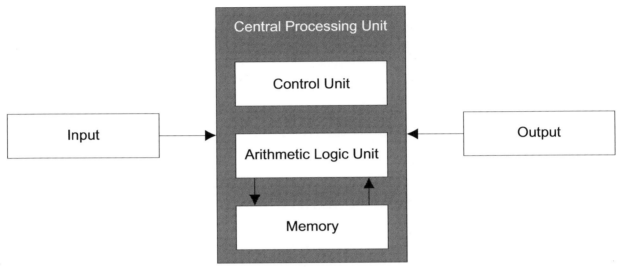

3.

4. Bus

5. (a) Regulates the timing and speed of all computer functions.
    (b) The speed of a clock is the number of vibrations a second. One megahertz is one million vibrations a second.

6. A CPU with two cores can execute two instructions at the same time, which can improve the performance of the CPU when performing certain tasks.
   Doubling the number of cores will not simply double a computer's speed. This is because software must be optimised to take advantage of multiple cores, and also because of the time taken in communicating between cores.

7. It is faster for the CPU to fetch data from and write it to the cache than to do so to/from Random Access Memory (RAM).
   The greater the size of the cache, the more data can be stored in cache rather than RAM, meaning that an increased cache size will improve the performance of the CPU.

8. Cache is graded as Level 1 (L1), Level 2 (L2) and Level 3 (L3): L1 is usually part of the CPU chip itself and is both the smallest and the fastest to access. Its size is often restricted to between 8 KB and 64 KB. L2 and L3 caches are bigger than L1. They are extra caches built between the CPU and the RAM. Sometimes L2 is built into the CPU with L1. L2 and L3 caches take slightly longer to access than L1. The more L2 and L3 memory available, the faster a computer can run.

9. Cloud storage is a type of off-site data storage provided and maintained by a third party hosting company. Data are stored on magnetic and solid state storage and can be stored across multiple servers and locations.

faster access	
cost effective	✓
full control of access to data	
10. scalable	✓
easily maintainable	✓
data safe from cyber attacks	
data safe from local problems, e.g. power cut at home/office	✓

11. (a) An embedded system is a computer system with hardware and software that is dedicated to performing a specific task within a bigger system.

(b) Any two of the following:

a kettle
a fridge
a car computer
an ATM (Automatic Teller Machine)
a mobile phone (not a smartphone)
a boiler
a washing machine
a satellite navigation system (sat nav)
a pair of Bluetooth earphones
any other sensible answer

12. (a) It is a general purpose computer system.

(b) Any two of the following:

a smartphone
a laptop
a personal computer
a server
a mainframe

13. (a) e.g. speed camera

(b) e.g. stock barcode scanner

(c) e.g. parking machine

(d) e.g. payment scanner

(e) e.g. lift

(f) e.g. ticket gate

14. Embedded systems perform specific tasks, whereas non-embedded systems are designed to be general purpose.
In embedded systems, it is normally not possible to upgrade hardware; software is often stored in non-volatile memory such as ROM, in which case it is difficult or impossible to upgrade.
Embedded systems are typically easier to use than non-embedded systems.

15. Any three of the following:

kettle
microwave
washing Machine

tumble dryer

electric oven

dishwasher

many other acceptable answers

16. E.g.:

Television – remote recording a programme

Central Heating system – controlled using an app on telephone

Smart meters – measuring gas, electricity, water

5   Networks

5.1   Network types and topologies

1. It is a network of computing devices, capable of sharing resources and transmitting data between devices.

2. Any three from:

sharing computing resources, e.g. printers, file server

reducing costs

easier communication between users of the same network

ability to manage security settings and software updates centrally

3. Any three from:

costly to set up

complexity of maintaining large networks

vulnerable to spread of malware

extra security procedures needed to protect from outside attack

4. (a) PAN (Personal Area Network) < LAN (Local Area Network) < WAN (Wide Area Network)

(b) For PAN, any two from:

used for connecting individual's personal devices

Bluetooth is a wireless example of PAN

USB is a wired example of PAN

For LAN, any two from:

used to cover a relatively small geographical area

normally controlled by a person or a small organisation

area of application can be within a home, school, or an office building

Ethernet or WiFi are used in a LAN

For WAN, any two from:

used to cover a big geographical area

normally controlled by big enterprises, education entities, service provides, or governments

the internet is a WAN

5. Any two from:

quick to connect new devices

convenience due to lack of cables

reduced cost in set up due to lack of cables

users have more freedom to move around whilst using the network

6. Any two from:

generally less secure

additional hardware required, e.g. wireless network interface cards

connections can be blocked by structures and items in the environment

potential liability of network owner for illegal activity of network users

7. (a) Bus topology and star topology

(b) For the bus topology:

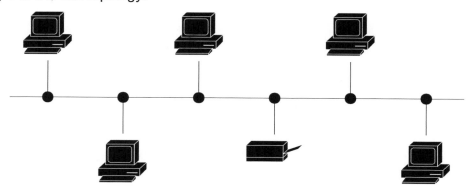

For the star topology:

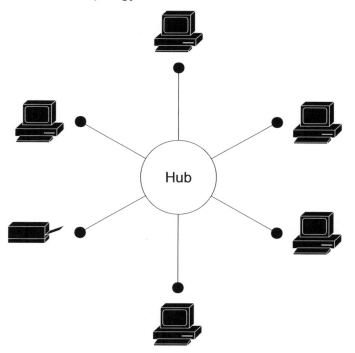

(c) Advantages of bus topology:

cheaper

simpler to set up

Advantages of star topology:

faster

simpler to add extra devices

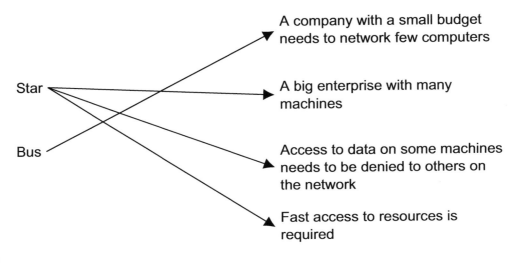

Star

Bus

A company with a small budget needs to network few computers

A big enterprise with many machines

Access to data on some machines needs to be denied to others on the network

Fast access to resources is required

8.

9. E.

5.2 Network protocols and TCP/IP

1. (a) A network protocol defines a set of rules for network devices to communicate with each other.

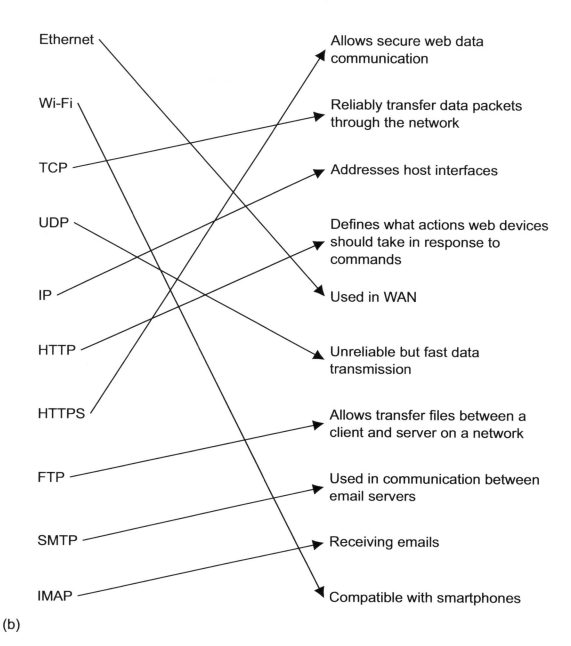

(b)

2. (a) application layer, transport layer, internet layer, link layer

(b) Any two of

application layer: where the network applications, e.g. web browsers or email programs, operate

transport layer: sets up and performs the communication between two network hosts

internet layer: addresses and packages data for network transmission and routes data across the network

link layer: where the network hardware, e.g. NIC (network interface card) or OS device drivers, operates

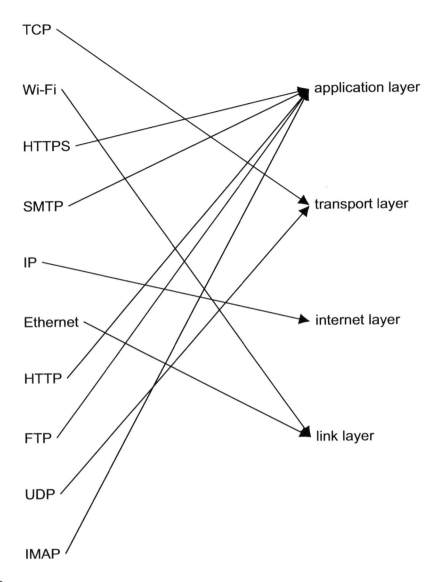

3.

5.3   Network security

1. Any two of:

   prevent and monitor unauthorised access to resources within a computer network

   prevent and monitor misuse of a computer network and its resources

   prevent and monitor attack of a computer network and its resources

2. Any two of:

   prevent costly repercussions to an organisation from a network breach

   prevent data loss resulting from attacks and misuse

   ensure data privacy

   restrict the sharing of resources to authorised users only

3. (a) Any two of:

   authentication

   authorisation

firewall

encryption

MAC address filtering

(b)   authentication: a procedure to ensure that a user is who they claim to be, for example by using a username and password or a biometric measure

authorisation: ensuring that resources are only accessible to those users with appropriate privilege

firewall: a device that blocks unexpected external traffic to or from a local network

encryption: changing data so that it is unreadable without a decryption key

MAC address filtering: restrict access to the network or its resources to specific devices based on MAC address, a physical address embedded within a device's network adapter

4. (a) A firewall blocks unauthorised network traffic between a local network and an external network such as the internet.

For example, a firewall might block a network user's attempt to access an insecure FTP server on the internet, or might block any attempt to remotely control a desktop PC to protect against misuse.

(b) MAC address filtering and a firewall working together can ensure that only known, local devices, can access the network, and all attempts to access the network remotely (e.g. from the internet) will be blocked.

Authentication adds an extra level of protection, as only those users with a valid username and password can access resources on the network.

The use of encryption ensures that even if any of the other methods fail, and data is stolen, it will be unreadable by an attacker.

5. A Media Access Control (MAC) address is a unique identifier embedded in every hardware device used on a computer network, consisting of six groups of two hexadecimal digits (or twelve hexadecimal digits). MAC address filtering works by either preventing or allowing a device to access a network based on its MAC address. MAC address filtering imposes restrictions on which hardware devices can access a network, rather than which users can.

6   Cyber security

6.1   Fundamentals of cyber security

1. Cyber security is the protection of computer systems from attack, damage, or unauthorised access. Different processes, practices and technologies are used to protect networks, computers, programs and data.

2. (a) Social engineering aims to manipulate computer system users to unintentionally give up confidential information, to gain access to sensitive computing data.

OR Social engineering is the art of manipulating people so they give up confidential information.

(b) Any two of:

username and password

National Insurance number

bank account details

date of birth

mother's maiden name

address

    (c) All of:

        blagging (or pretexting)

        phishing

        pharming

        shouldering (or shoulder surfing)

3. Any two of

    use strong passwords

    only give out sensitive information to trusted individuals

    use secure networks and visit secure websites (i.e. those using HTTPS and using a verified security certificate)

    do not open unverified documents, links, or attachments to unsolicited emails

    use up-to-date antivirus software

4. Blagging is using an invented scenario to persuade victims to reveal private information, or to perform actions that compromise their network security.

5. Phishing is a technique of fraudulently obtaining private information by crafting an electronic communication (e.g. email or SMS) that appears to come from a legitimate sender (such as a bank).

6. Pharming involves creating a fake website that mimics a legitimate company's website, to try obtain confidential information (for example, login details for the legitimate website).

7. Shouldering is observing a person's private information over their shoulder e.g. cashpoint machine PIN.

8. (a) Malware is an umbrella term used to refer to a variety of forms of hostile or intrusive software.

    (b) Any two of

        use up-to-date anti-virus software

        use a firewall that only allows connections to/from an external network that meet certain criteria

        adjust browser security settings to prevent untrusted applications from being launched

        never open attachments to emails from unknown or untrusted senders

        only download software from trusted websites

        read reviews / small print to check that applications are free from adware

    (c) All of

        computer virus

        Trojan (Trojan horse)

        spyware

        adware

9. A computer virus is a type of malware that replicates itself and spreads without the direct involvement of the computer's user.

10. A Trojan is a type of malware that disguises itself as a legitimate computer program or document, tricking the user to open it. Once opened, malicious code is executed.

11. Spyware is a type of malware that monitors and stores data about a user's use of a computer. A keylogger is an example of spyware. It can be deployed by companies or malicious attackers to track user behaviour.

12. Adware is a type of malware that displays unwanted advertisements to computer users.

13. Any four of:

> social engineering techniques
>
> malicious code
>
> weak and default passwords
>
> misconfigured access rights
>
> removable media
>
> unpatched and/or outdated software

14. Any plausible scenario that describes misconfigured access rights and their threat consequence will be accepted: Having a weak password, e.g. "password", to a company admin account. Unauthorised user can log in and modify company employee information stored, e.g. name, salary etc.

15. Removable media including USB sticks and mobile smart devices increase the chance of loss and misplacement of data if users are not careful.
    In the case of malicious attacks, an attacker can steal data from an organisation easily with removable media.
    Since these devices are connected directly to computer hardware within the local network, security measures intended to protect the network are bypassed, therefore malware can be introduced to a network more easily via such devices.

6.2 Preventing cyber security threats

1. (a) Penetration testing is a security test in which the tester attempts to gain access to resources without knowledge of usernames, passwords and other normal means of access.
   (b) Both of:

   > white-box penetration testing
   > black-box penetration testing

2. (a) A white-box penetration tester tries simulate a malicious insider who has knowledge of and possibly basic credentials for a target system.
   (b) Name any of the social engineering methods:

   > blagging
   > phishing
   > pharming
   > shouldering

   or, name any of the network security threats:

   > social engineering techniques
   > malicious code
   > weak and default passwords
   > misconfigured access rights
   > removable media
   > unpatched and/or outdated software

3. (a) A black-box penetration tester simulates an external hacker or cyber warfare attacker.
   (b) Name any of the social engineering methods:

   > blagging
   > phishing
   > pharming

shouldering

or, name any of the network security threats:

social engineering techniques
malicious code
weak and default passwords
misconfigured access rights
removable media
unpatched and/or outdated software

4. (a) Any one of:

difficult to steal a biometric characteristic
difficult to lose a biometric characteristic

(b) Any one of:

can be unreliable at times
more complicated implementation than password
can be inconvenient because tied to individual characteristics

(c) Any three of:

fingerprint recognition
voice recognition
face recognition
signature recognition
iris recognition
retinal recognition

5. Any three of

biometric measures (particularly for mobile devices)

password systems

CAPTCHA

using email confirmations to confirm a user's identity

automatic software updates

6. CAPTCHA is a type of test used in computing to check whether the user is a human, and reject attempts by robots to access resources. It requires the user to type out an obscured or distorted set of letters or digits correctly, a task that is very difficult for a computer to complete successfully.

7   Ethics, the law and the environment

7.1   Ethical issues

1. (a) Any two of:

it is easier to detect fraud based on past legal and financial history
it is more straightforward to approve loans based on good past credit history
ratings from family and friends could help to decide if it is safe to meet someone online
it has the potential to improve efficiency in legal procedures like tackling corruption and sentencing
it has the potential to improve efficiency in financial procedures like buying a new house and getting loans approved

government could be better able to protect citizens from criminals (e.g. counterfeiters, corrupt officials, terrorists) when they have access to personal data

(b) Any two of:

ordinary citizens value their privacy and do not like government, companies or other individuals to have too much access to their private data

"good" and "bad" behaviour used for scoring in such a system could easily be based on the biased views of individuals who designed the system

the system might not allow people to make mistakes in life without it permanently affecting their scores

the pressure of living life in a way that maintains a good score could impact individuals' mental and emotional well being

living near, or being related to, people with bad scores could impact an individual's score unfairly.

it could be very difficult to improve a bad score.

(c) Any two of:

the way of measuring "good" and "bad" behaviour in a wide range of areas could be poorly defined and regulated

the total impact on an individual's score from many minor offences, like speeding tickets or bad borrowing habits, could be the same as from one major offence, like murder or robbery. It would be unfair because without context, both could affect this individual's future treatment in the same way

a citizen's right to privacy can be compromised when private data are being used to generate the score. Government might be able to access any data for reasons that it sees fit

any cheating or corruption in the system might be difficult to detect once the data collected has been reduced to a single score

2. (a) For example: Sharing a journey between multiple passengers reduces fuel consumption per passenger.
Sharing a car means fewer vehicles need to be produced, reducing the natural resources and energy used in making them.

(b) For example:

The cyber security of these vehicles' computer systems needs to be regulated and guaranteed. The legal penalty of hacking a vehicle's computer system must be determined.

Legal guidelines for determining the responsible party in the event of an accident must be established. Is it the vehicle handler, the vehicle owner, the developer of the computer systems, the vehicle manufacturer or should it be determined on a case by case basis?

The legal responsibility of the people handling the vehicles must be determined. What things are they allowed to do (e.g. reading, eating, watch videos etc) whilst being in charge of the vehicle? Should a passenger be considered responsible for the vehicle and its actions?

3. (a) Hacking is the attempt to break into a computer or network system without authorisation to explore the weaknesses of the system.

(b) Cracking is the attempt to break into a computer or network system without authorisation, with criminal intent.

Often break things

Usually knowledgeable about
computer and internet security

Relies on existing tools to break   Cracker
into computer systems

Breaks into systems for criminal
intentions

Find weaknesses in computer
security systems

Able to improve a computer system

Prevent crimes committed against   Hacker
a system

Usually able to write computer
programs

Exploit flaws in a computer system

(c)

4. (a) Any two of:

record physical activities data like walking, running, allowing statistical analysis and
progress tracking

measure and monitor health metrics, like blood pressure, sleeping pattern and heart
rates; these could be useful for regulating health issues, or the detection and prevention of illnesses

wearable technologies on pets can allow owners to be aware of the whereabouts of
their pets

Virtual Reality (VR) headsets are used to create a more stimulating and realistic environment for individuals to play games, athletes to train more flexibly and some safety
drills to be conducted more easily

medical wearable technology like smart hearing aids are provide more options to cus-
tomise to individual needs than a conventional device would

(b) Ethical or legal concerns could be:

malicious attacks can happen and subject users to privacy invasion and spamming

malicious attacks can happen and subject users to financial loss

malicious attacks can happen and subject users to blackmail

carelessness can result in data being exposed to unwanted parties

inadequate backup measures could result in data being lost

since technology companies can decide how the collected data is used, users can be
vulnerable to exploitation

(c) i. Any one of:

less likely to lose implanted devices

precision in recording medical data and history

theft prevention: harder to steal than external objects

users can benefit from the implant without having to worry about installing / activating it, e.g. better hearing from a cochlear implant

ii. Any one of:

uncertain long term physical health impact from the materials used in making the implants

uncertain long term mental health impact from people living with smart devices embedded within their bodies

future technological improvement would require modification, removal or addition of the implants' hardware which would, therefore, require further medical procedures

poor regulatory guidelines and legal measures means difficult to track down accountability when something goes wrong

an implant's vulnerability to a malicious attacker, or the presence of bugs, could have unintended consequences to patients with implants

5. (a) Copyright gives the authors of a computer program the right to define how they want their program to be used.

(b) Any three of:

copying

modifying

buying

lending

renting

licensing

distributing/sharing

(c) Open source software authors allow others to use, copy, edit and share the software, but users must comply with any conditions listed in the software's licence (e.g. that the licence text is included when the software is shared, or that any user modficiations are made available under the original licence).

6. Some accepted points:

An algorithm is a sequence of steps that can be followed to complete a task, it is non-specific. Copyright protects a specific creative expression of an idea.

In a computer program, copyright protection is limited to the specific implementation of an algorithm, so in general, the algorithm itself cannot be copyrighted.

An exception to this is that if an algorithm can only be expressed in one way, then it can be subject to copyright. Any complicated algorithm is unlikely to fit that exception.

7. (a) Any three of:

backup of personal data

backup of company data

storage of old data

storage of less frequently used data

storage of data that takes up a lot of memory locally

(b) Some acceptable points:

cloud providers can manage energy consumption more efficiently

providers combine computing processes on the same servers

combined running in turn reduce the number of servers needed and has less impact on the energy used

investments on the more advanced cooling system would improve energy consumption

(c) Any two of:

depending on the terms and conditions of the service, users might not have the legal right to access or move data, or the provider might have legal ownership of the data

important to determine who has legal liability for the loss or theft of the data

check the security measure that cloud providers have put in place to prevent loss of data via different means: security breach, power loss etc.

check the measures cloud providers have put in to ensure continual of service and if there are compensation in place if loss of service has caused any financial or social impact

8. (a) If Alex takes any code from the old company and use it in the new company, he would have committed software theft.

(b) If Bethany plays the copied games with the simulator program, she would have committed software theft.

(c) If Charlie access beyond the point where the trial ends, he would have committed software theft.

(d) If Duncan does not comply with the licence for the open source software, or claims that the code he has used is his own, he would have committed software theft.

9. Points can include:

people struggle to switch off from out of hours notifications, from emails, chats, news, social media updates, causing mental and physical exhaustion

people more easily develop addictions toward gambling, games, social media, streaming services etc, leading to an unbalanced lifestyle, excluding activities outside of technology

social media impacts self esteem and projects unhealthy and unrealistic expectations of life, leading to increased cases of mental health problems

mobile technology increases exposure of potentially vulnerable people to the internet. Children and adults with less experience of technology can be exposed to material that is inappropriate, or can have their privacy unexpectedly violated, or fall victim to fraud.

misinformation accessible from the internet via mobile technologies can spread very rapidly and widely

mobile technologies allow sensitive information about individuals or organisations to be misplaced, leaked and lost very easily. Even if cyber security measures must be in place to protect data on mobile devices, human error will still be a vulnerability

10. (a) Valid answers include:

restaurants

underground/metro/train ticket gates

ticket machines

buses

(b) Valid answers include:

mobile phones

smart watches

credit and debit cards

tablets

(c) i. For card payments, there is a £30 limit per transaction. Retailers sometimes set a limit too.

ii. Payment machines are programmed to not accept multiple payments from the same card for the same amount at around the same time.

iii. Banks would not authorise payments resulting from fraudulent usage as long as any loss or theft was reported promptly.

11. (a) Valid points include:

convenience and reduced cost encourage people to use air and road travel more, this increases energy usage and air pollution

people use more energy due to the benefits brought about by technological advancement, e.g. people watch more television, keep mobile devices and computing devices on

affordability and frequent production of new models means people buy new devices and discard old ones in short periods of time, creating massive amounts of e-waste

improved methods in construction accelerate the building of cities and this has a negative impact on the environment

improved methods in agriculture increase the rate of food production, cost resources to produce the food and can lead to food waste

(b) Valid points include:

developing alternative food source that requires less raw materials to grow or raise

technology developed to enable more usage of renewable energy, like wind, solar and hydropower

newer technology developed to use energy more efficiently comparing to previous models, e.g. electric cars

better sorting and disassembling of electronics allow parts to be recycled and reused

technology can be used to reduce pollution and improve air quality

smart technologies used at home and in offices have the potential to reduce energy usage

online and mobile technologies reduces the need to use as much paper and ink

Printed in Great Britain
by Amazon

34925552R00063